D1262110

HOW DOES IT FLY?

# HELICOPTER

BY MATT MULLINS

Published in the United States of America by Cherry Lake Publishing
Ann Arbor, Michigan
www.cherrylakepublishing.com

Content Adviser: Jacob Zeiger, Production Support Engineer, the Boeing Company

Photo Credits: Cover and page 1, ©PhotoStock-Israel/Alamy; page 5, ©Christopher Dodge/Shutterstock, Inc.; page 7, ©Kayros Studio "Be Happy!"/Shutterstock, Inc.; page 9, ©AP PHOTO/Fritz Reiss; page 11, ©Kameel4u/Shutterstock, Inc.; page 13, ©iStockphoto.com/mikadx; page 15, ©ericlefrancais/Shutterstock, Inc.; page 17, ©David Hancock/Shutterstock, Inc.; page 19, ©Mikhail Blajenov/Dreamstime.com; page 21, ©Tony Hobbs/Alamy.



**LIBRARY OF CONGRESS CATALOGING-IN-PUBLICATION DATA**
Mullins, Matt.
How does it fly? Helicopter/by Matt Mullins.
p. cm.—(Community connections)
Includes bibliographical references and index.
ISBN-13: 978-1-61080-065-5 (library binding)
ISBN-10: 1-61080-065-6 (library binding)
1. Helicopters—Juvenile literature. I. Title. II. Title: Helicopter.
III. Series.
TL716.2.M85 2011
629.133'352—dc22 2010051584

Cherry Lake Publishing would like to acknowledge the work of The Partnership for 21st Century Skills. Please visit *www.21stcenturyskills.org* for more information.

Printed in the United States of America
Corporate Graphics Inc.
July 2011
CLFA09

# CONTENTS



HOW DOES IT FLY?

# SPECIAL FLYING MACHINES

Sometimes you feel it before you see it. You hear thumping in the air. Then you see it come around the trees or tall buildings.
Its blades are whirling.
It is a helicopter!

A helicopter flies over the River Thames in London.

Helicopters do things planes cannot. They take off and land in small places. They can move backward, forward, sideways, or even straight up. They can hover in place. Many of them can carry heavy things, such as houses and radio towers.

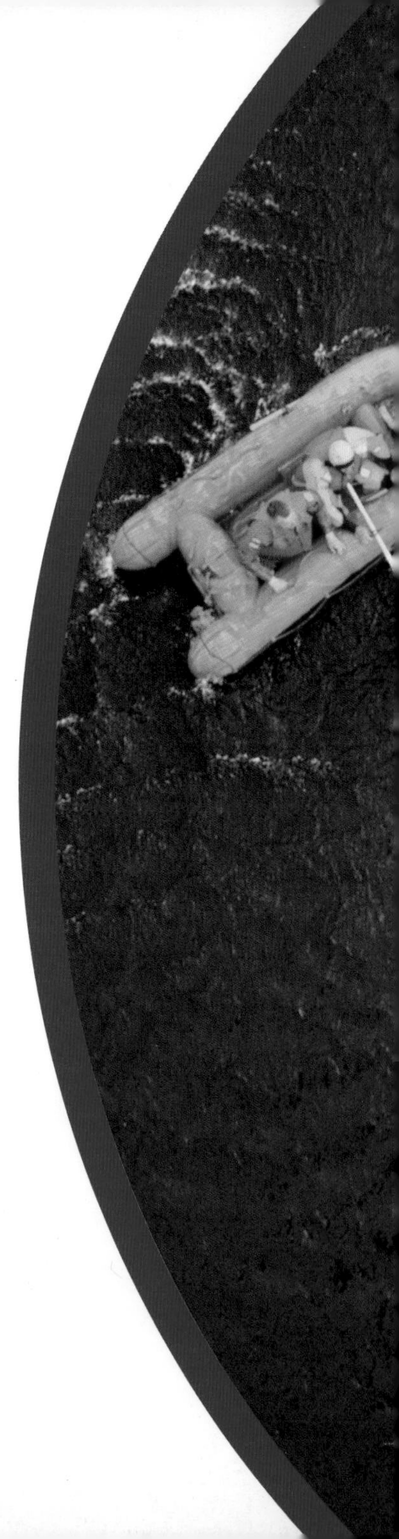



Helicopters can hover above someone in need of rescue. This makes it easier for rescuers to reach the person.

## CREATE!

Make a list of things that helicopters can do. Create a list for planes, too. Think of how we save people from floods or fires. Can planes do that? Which flying machine has the longer list?

# FROM ANCIENT TO MODERN TIMES

More than 2,000 years ago, Chinese children played with toys that worked like helicopters. The toys rose into the air when spun.

In 1483 Leonardo da Vinci drew a flying machine. It had a large, screw-shaped blade that would pull it into the air.



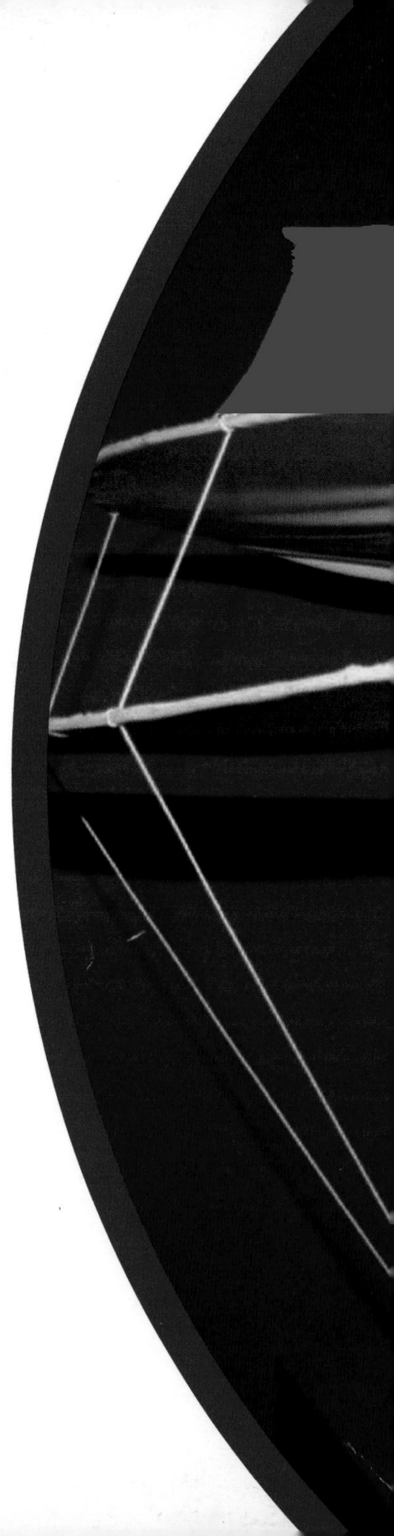

Da Vinci's helicopter never flew, but museums sometimes display models of the machine.

In 1907, France's Paul Cornu invented a helicopter. It was the first one that could be controlled while flying. It had two wide blades. They swung in circles on a **rotor**. Cornu attached one rotor to each end of his machine. His first flight held him 12 inches (30 centimeters) in the air for 20 seconds.

Today's helicopters still fly using blades that turn on rotors.

CREW

In 1940 Russian-American **engineer** Igor Sikorsky flew his own helicopter. One large rotor was located behind the pilot's seat. A smaller rotor was attached to the machine's tail.

Sikorsky flew his machine backward, up, down, and sideways. Eventually, he was also able to fly forward!

These Black Hawk helicopters were made by the company founded by Igor Sikorsky.

## MAKE A GUESS!

A helicopter's blades work like a plane's wings. They are shaped so air gives the helicopter **lift**. The spinning rotor also provides **thrust**. This moves the helicopter through the air. Can you guess how a helicopter moves in different directions?

# PARTS AND TYPES OF HELICOPTERS

Today, the helicopter's pilot and passengers sit in the **fuselage**. The rotor and engine are usually behind the passenger area. A helicopter's **boom** trails out from the fuselage like a tail. A tail rotor helps steer the machine. **Landing skids** work like feet.



Can you find all the parts of the helicopter?

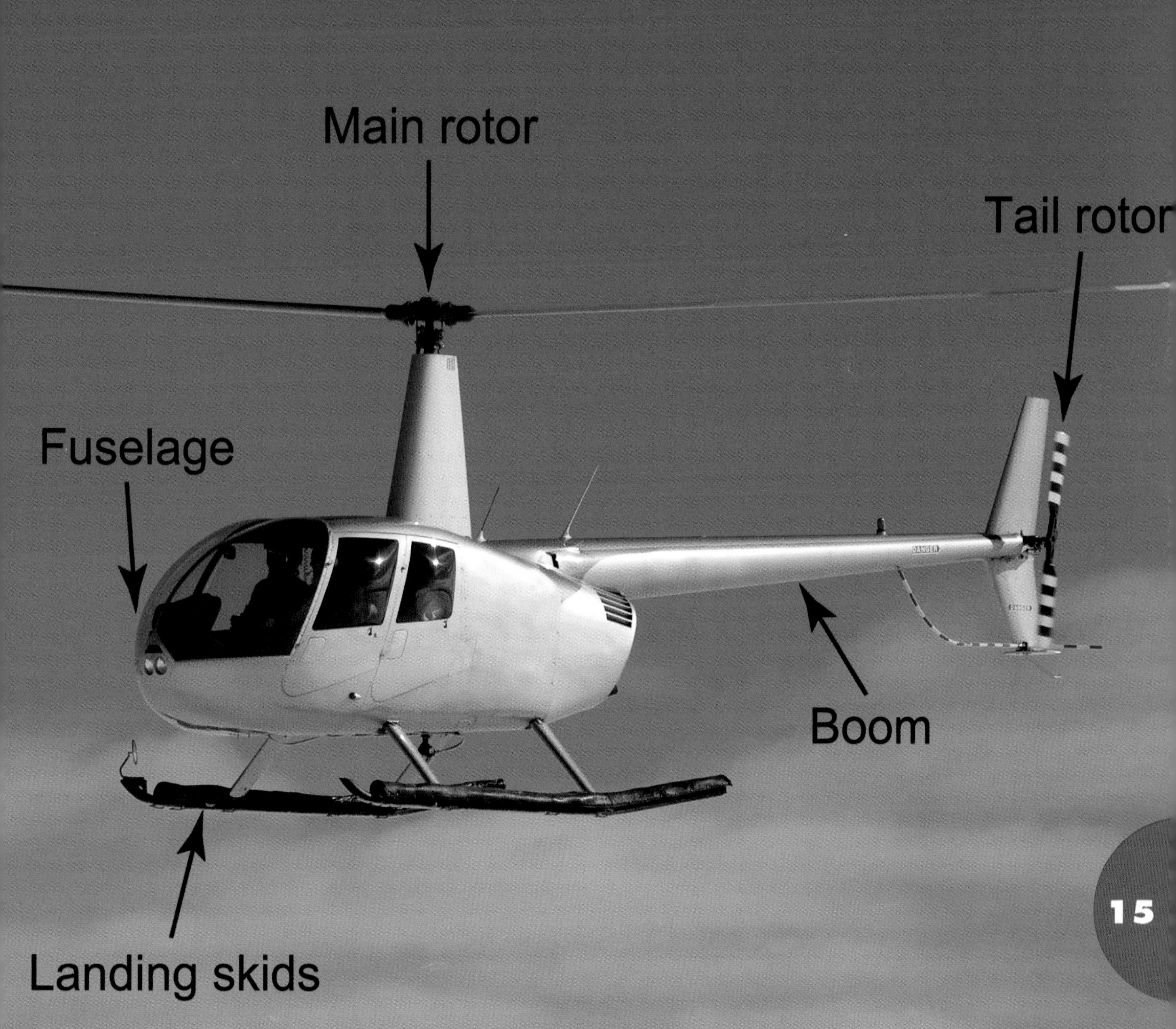
Main rotor
Tail rotor
Fuselage
Boom
Landing skids

There are many kinds of helicopters. Helicopter cranes lift heavy things. These helicopters usually have long thin bodies like dragonflies. **Air ambulances** bring sick people to hospitals.

Helicopters are used for chasing criminals, fertilizing crops, and fighting fires. Attack helicopters with big guns can even shoot **missiles**.

An air ambulance lifts off from the scene of a car accident.

## THINK!

Helicopters are constantly being improved. Engineers design more powerful engines or new blades, rotors, or fuselages. What changes do you think might be made to helicopters in the future? What new uses will there be for helicopters?

# THE FUTURE FOR HELICOPTERS

Helicopter design will continue to change. More helicopters are using two sets of blades instead of one. They spin in opposite directions. This makes a helicopter easier to control. The smaller tail rotor can then be used for thrust. This allows a helicopter to travel faster.

The Kamov-52 has one set of blades located directly above the other set.

Some new helicopters have wings with engines, similar to a plane. These increase speed and lift.

For decades, people have hoped that helicopters would become as common as cars. Can you imagine? Maybe someday we will park helicopters outside our houses!



The Bell/Agusta 609's rotors can point up, for lift, or forward, for thrust.

## LOOK!

The next time you see a helicopter, take a good look at it. Does it seem big or little? How big is its tail rotor? Can you tell what the helicopter might be used for?

# GLOSSARY

**air ambulances** (AYR AM-byoo-lunss-iz) helicopters that carry sick or injured people

**boom** (BOOM) a long piece that sticks out behind the fuselage of a helicopter

**engineer** (en-juh-NEER) a person who designs or builds structures and machines

**fuselage** (FEW-suh-lahdj) center part of an aircraft where the crew, passengers, and cargo sit

**landing skids** (LAN-ding SKIDZ) rails under the fuselage that the helicopter stands on when landed

**lift** (LIFT) the upward force of flight

**missiles** (MISS-uhlz) weapons that are fired, thrown, dropped, or flown toward a target

**rotor** (ROH-tur) spinning blades and shaft

**thrust** (THRUHST) the forward force of flight

# FIND OUT MORE

## BOOKS

Eason, Sarah. *How Does a Helicopter Work?* New York: Gareth Stevens Publishing, 2010.

Von Finn, Denny. *Military Helicopters*. Minneapolis: Bellwether Media, 2010.

Wyckoff, Edwin Brit. *Helicopter Man: Igor Sikorsky and His Amazing Invention*. Berkeley Heights, NJ: Enslow Publishers, 2010.

## WEB SITES

**Helicopter History Site**
*www.helis.com/*
Find videos, audios, games, activities, and more about helicopters.

**NASA—Robin Whirlybird on her Rotorcraft Adventures**
*http://rotored.arc.nasa.gov/index.html*
Stories, history, and activities about a girl and helicopters.

# INDEX



## ABOUT THE AUTHOR

Matt Mullins lives near an airport in Madison, Wisconsin. Matt has a master's degree in the history of science and writes about all sorts of things—science, technology, business, academics, food, and more. He also writes and directs films and spends time with his son.